THE 30-MINUTE SHAKESPEARE
THE TAMING OF THE SHREW

"Nick Newlin's work as a teaching artist for Folger Education during the past thirteen years has provided students, regardless of their experience with Shakespeare or being on stage, a unique opportunity to tread the boards at the Folger Theatre. Working with students to edit Shakespeare's plays for performance at the annual Folger Shakespeare Festivals has enabled students to gain new insights into the Bard's plays, build their skills of comprehension and critical reading, and just plain have fun working collaboratively with their peers.

Folger Education promotes performance-based teaching of Shakespeare's plays, providing students with an interactive approach to Shakespeare's plays in which they participate in a close reading of the text through intellectual, physical, and vocal engagement. Newlin's *The 30-Minute Shakespeare* series is an invaluable resource for teachers of Shakespeare, and for all who are interested in performing the plays."

ROBERT YOUNG, PH.D.
DIRECTOR OF EDUCATION
FOLGER SHAKESPEARE LIBRARY

The Taming of the Shrew: The 30-Minute Shakespeare
ISBN 978-1-935550-33-4
Adaptation, essays, and notes ©2018 by Nick Newlin

Cover design by Sarah Juckniess
Printed in the United States of America

Distributed by Consortium Book Sales & Distribution
www.cbsd.com

NICOLO WHIMSEY PRESS
www.30MinuteShakespeare.com

Art Director: Sarah Juckniess
Managing Editors: Katherine Little, Leah Gordon

A PLEASANT CONCEITED HISTORIE
CALLED

THE TAMING
OF THE SHREW

THE 30-MINUTE SHAKESPEARE

Written by **WILLIAM SHAKESPEARE**

Abridged AND Edited
by **NICK NEWLIN**

Nicolo Whimsey
Press

Brandywine, MD

To my grandfather
E. Mortimer Newlin
("Grampa")

Who loved
a good laugh

Special thanks to Joanne Flynn, Bill Newlin, Eliza Newlin Carney, William and Louisa Newlin, Michael Tolaydo, Hilary Kacser, Sarah Juckniess, Katherine Little, Eva Zimmerman, Leah Gordon, Tanya Tolchin, Frank Harris, Julie Schaper and all of Consortium, Leo Bowman and the students, faculty, and staff at Banneker Academic High School, Charlie Feeser, and Robert Young Ph.D. and the Folger Shakespeare Library, especially the wonderful Education Department.

✳ TABLE OF CONTENTS

✳ NO EXPERIENCE NECESSARY

I was not a big "actor type" in high school, so if you weren't either, or if the young people you work with are not, then this book is for you. Whether or not you work with "actor types," you can use this book to stage a lively and captivating thirty-minute version of a Shakespeare play. No experience is necessary.

When I was about eleven years old, my parents took me to see Shakespeare's *Two Gentlemen of Verona*, which was being performed as a Broadway musical. I didn't comprehend every word I heard, but I was enthralled with the language, the characters, and the story, and I understood enough of it to follow along. From then on, I associated Shakespeare with *fun*.

Of course Shakespeare is fun. The Elizabethan audiences knew it, which is one reason he was so popular. It didn't matter that some of the language eluded them. The characters were passionate and vibrant, and their conflicts were compelling. Young people study Shakespeare in high school, but more often than not they read his work like a text book and then get quizzed on academic elements of the play, such as plot, theme, and vocabulary. These are all very interesting, but not nearly as interesting as standing up and performing a scene! It is through performance that the play comes alive and all its "academic" elements are revealed. There is nothing more satisfying to a student or teacher than the feeling of "owning" a Shakespeare play, and that can only come from performing it.

But Shakespeare's plays are often two or more hours long, making the performance of an entire play almost out of the question. One can perform a single scene, which is certainly a good start, but what about the story? What about the changes a character goes through as the play progresses? When school groups perform one scene unedited, or when they lump several plays together, the audience can get lost. This is why I have always preferred to tell the story of the play.

The 30-Minute Shakespeare gives students and teachers a chance to get up on their feet and act out a Shakespeare play in half an hour, using his language. The emphasis is on key scenes, with narrative bridges between scenes to keep the audience caught up on the action. The stage directions are built into this script so that young actors do not have to stand in one place; they can move and tell the story with their actions as well as their words. And it can all be done in a classroom during class time!

That is where this book was born: not in a research library, a graduate school lecture, a professional stage, or even an after-school drama club. All of the play cuttings in *The 30-Minute Shakespeare* were first rehearsed in a D.C. public high school English class, and performed successfully at the Folger Shakespeare Library's annual Secondary School Shakespeare Festival. The players were not necessarily "actor types." For many of them, this was their first performance in a play.

Something almost miraculous happens when students perform Shakespeare. They "get" it. By occupying the characters and speaking the words out loud, students gain a level of understanding and appreciation that is unachievable by simply reading the text. That is the magic of a performance-based method of learning Shakespeare, and this book makes the formerly daunting task of staging a Shakespeare play possible for anybody.

With *The 30-Minute Shakespeare* book series I hope to help teachers and students produce a Shakespeare play in a short amount of time, thus jump-starting the process of discovering the beauty, magic, and fun of the Bard. Plot, theme, and language reveal themselves through the performance of these half-hour play cuttings, and everybody involved receives the priceless gift of "owning" a piece of Shakespeare. The result is an experience that is fun and engaging, and one that we can all carry with us as we play out our own lives on the stages of the world.

NICK NEWLIN
Brandywine, MD
March 2010

CHARACTERS IN THE PLAY

The following is a list of characters that appear in this cutting of *The Taming of the Shrew*.

Sixteen actors appeared in the original production. The number can be increased to about thirty or decreased to about ten by having actors share or double roles.

For the full breakdown of characters, see Sample Program.

LUCENTIO: Suitor to Bianca, later disguised as the teacher Cambio

TRANIO: Servant to Lucentio

BAPTISTA: Father to Katherine and Bianca

GREMIO: Suitor to Bianca

KATHERINE: Baptista's elder daughter

BIANCA: Baptista's younger daughter

PETRUCHIO: Suitor to Katherine

GRUMIO: Servant to Petruchio

HORTENSIO: Suitor to Bianca, later disguised as the teacher Litio

BIONDELLO: Servant to Lucentio

WIDOW

SERVANTS

CHORUS MEMBERS

NARRATOR

✳ SCENE 1. (ACT I, SCENE I)

Padua, the town square.

STAGEHANDS *set two benches stage right and two benches stage left, side by side and facing center stage. Each bench holds four actors. Prior to curtain, the individual actors will place their props below the bench on which they will be sitting.*

Enter **ALL,** *excluding* **LUCENTIO, TRANIO, BIONDELLO, PETRUCHIO, GREMIO, BIANCA, BAPTISTA,** *and* **KATHERINE,** *dancing, waving, and playing instruments. They circle the stage and then sit, four actors to a bench. All cast members return to their respective benches throughout the play rather than exiting offstage. While on the benches, the cast serves as the* **CHORUS,** *sometimes leaping up to participate and then returning to their benches.*

Enter **LUCENTIO** *and* **TRANIO** *separately, walking in from stage left.*

LUCENTIO

> Tranio, my trusty servant,
> To see fair Padua,

ALL *onstage cheer.*

> I am arrived.
> But stay awhile! What company is this?

TRANIO

> Master, some show to welcome us to town.

SOUND OPERATOR *plays Sound Cue #1 ("Drumroll").*

ALL *look stage right.*

Enter BIONDELLO, PETRUCHIO, *and* GREMIO *from stage right, looking frightened.* GREMIO *is using a cane. A shoe is thrown at them from offstage right.*

Enter BIANCA *from stage right, running and ducking from an object being thrown from offstage. A shoe comes flying out, and she ducks. She nearly runs into* BIONDELLO, PETRUCHIO, *and* GREMIO, *but they catch her. As soon as* BIANCA *enters,* LUCENTIO *can't keep his eyes off her.*

Another shoe is thrown from offstage right.

Enter BAPTISTA *from stage right, walking backward with his arms in front of him, protecting himself.* ALL *look at* BAPTISTA, *put their arms out in front of them, and gaze expectantly stage right. Nothing happens.*

SOUND OPERATOR *plays* Sound Cue #2 *("Drumroll").*

From offstage right, another shoe is thrown. ALL *watch as it bounces across the stage.*

Enter KATHERINE *from stage right. Her hair looks wild, and she is glaring. She stands center stage, takes a few threatening steps toward the front row, and scowls.*

ALL *onstage yell in terror.*

KATHERINE *moves toward* BAPTISTA, BIANCA, TRANIO, *and* BIONDELLO.

HORTENSIO *makes his way toward the crowd, staring at* BIANCA.

LUCENTIO *eyes* HORTENSIO *suspiciously as he notices that* HORTENSIO *desires* BIANCA.

BAPTISTA *(to* GREMIO *and* HORTENSIO*)*
Gentlemen, I firmly am resolved
not to bestow my youngest daughter
Before I have a husband for the elder.
If either of you both love Katherine

ALL *back away one step and yell in fear.*

Leave shall you have to court her at your pleasure.

GREMIO *(slowly backing away)*
She's too rough for me.

KATHERINE *(to* BAPTISTA*)*
Is it your will
To make a stale of me amongst these mates?

HORTENSIO
No mates for you,
Unless you were of gentler, milder mold.

KATHERINE *(to* HORTENSIO*)*
Her care should be
To comb your noddle with a three-legged stool.

KATHERINE *grabs* GREMIO'S *cane and threatens to hit* HORTENSIO *with it.*

GREMIO *almost falls down. He grabs onto* HORTENSIO *to keep himself upright.*

GREMIO *and* HORTENSIO *both back away from* KATHERINE.

HORTENSIO
From all such devils, good Lord, deliver us!

GREMIO
> And me too, good Lord.

TRANIO *(aside to* LUCENTIO*)*
> That wench is stark mad or wonderful froward.

LUCENTIO *(aside to* TRANIO, *gazing at* BIANCA*)*
> But in the other's silence do I see
> Maid's mild behavior and sobriety.
> Peace, Tranio.

TRANIO *(aside to* LUCENTIO*)*
> Well said, master, and gaze your fill.

BAPTISTA *(gesturing upstage rear)*
> Bianca, get you in.

KATHERINE
> A pretty peat!

BIANCA
> Sister, content you in my discontent.
> Sir, to your pleasure humbly I subscribe.

Exit BIANCA *to bench.*

BAPTISTA
> Katherine, you may stay,
> For I have more to commune with Bianca.

ALL *onstage say, "Aww," reacting to* BIANCA'S *cuteness.*

BIANCA *stands blushingly, with a little curtsy, and then sits back down on her bench.*

Exit BAPTISTA *to his bench, taking* BIANCA *with him.*

KATHERINE
> I may go too, may I not? Ha!

Exit KATHERINE *to her bench. Before leaving, she stops, turns around, lunges toward group onstage, and roars.*

ALL *onstage yell in terror.*

GREMIO
> You may go to the devil's dam!

HORTENSIO
> There's small choice in rotten
> apples. By helping Baptista's eldest daughter
> to a husband we set his youngest free for a husband.
> Sweet Bianca!

ALL *onstage swoon and say, "Aww."*

BIANCA *stands to reprise her blush and curtsy, then sits back down.*

> He that runs fastest gets the ring.
> How say you, Signior Gremio?

GREMIO
> I am agreed. Come on.

Exit GREMIO *and* HORTENSIO *to their benches.*

TRANIO *and* LUCENTIO *come center stage.*

TRANIO
> I pray, sir, tell me, is it possible
> That love should of a sudden take such hold?

LUCENTIO (*gazing over audience, thinking of* BIANCA)
    Tranio, I saw her coral lips to move,
    And with her breath she did perfume the air.

TRANIO (*to audience*)
    Nay, then 'tis time to stir him from his trance.

TRANIO *snaps his fingers in front of* LUCENTIO'S *eyes. There is no response.* TRANIO *claps his hands.*

    I pray, awake, sir!
    Her elder sister is so curst and shrewd
    That till the father rid his hands of her,
    Master, your love must live a maid at home.

LUCENTIO
    But art thou not advised he took some care
    To get her cunning schoolmasters to instruct her?

TRANIO (*thinking*)
    Ay, marry, am I, sir—and now 'tis plotted!
    You will be schoolmaster
    And undertake the teaching of the maid.
    Take my colored hat and cloak.

LUCENTIO *and* TRANIO *exchange clothes and exit to their benches.*

✳ **SCENE 2.** (ACT I, SCENE II)

Padua, the town square.

Stage right are a FRUIT VENDOR *and a* FLOWER VENDOR.

Stage left are a WIDOW *and the* WIDOW'S DATE.

Stage left center is HORTENSIO, *dozing in a chair.*

Enter PETRUCHIO *and his man* GRUMIO *from stage rear.* GRUMIO *carries* PETRUCHIO'S *bag.*

PETRUCHIO *grabs a flower from the* FLOWER VENDOR'S *basket. She tries to stop him, but he keeps moving. While the* FRUIT VENDOR *and the* FLOWER VENDOR *are watching* PETRUCHIO, GRUMIO *grabs an apple from the* FRUIT VENDOR'S *basket.*

PETRUCHIO *gives the flower to the* WIDOW, *who blushes.*

The WIDOW'S DATE *becomes flustered, buys a bunch of flowers from the* FLOWER VENDOR, *and gives them to the* WIDOW.

Meanwhile, PETRUCHIO *walks stage left to where* HORTENSIO *is napping.*

PETRUCHIO *(to* GRUMIO*)*
> Verona, for a while I take my leave
> To see in Padua

ALL *onstage and offstage cheer with the exception of* PETRUCHIO, GRUMIO, *and* HORTENSIO.

My best beloved friend, Hortensio.
Here, sirrah Grumio, knock, I say.

GRUMIO *looks around, confused, and holds his fists up, ready to fight.*

GRUMIO
Knock, sir? Whom should I knock? Is there
any man has rebused your Worship?

PETRUCHIO
Villain, I say, knock me here soundly.

GRUMIO
Knock you here, sir?

GRUMIO *looks around him, glances at audience, shrugs, and winds up as if to punch* PETRUCHIO.

PETRUCHIO *sees what* GRUMIO *is about to do and grabs him by the ears.*

PETRUCHIO
Villain, I say, knock me at this gate
And rap me well, or I'll knock your knave's pate.

PETRUCHIO *wrings* GRUMIO *by the ears.*

GRUMIO *falls.*

GRUMIO *(to audience, complaining)*
My master is grown quarrelsome.

PETRUCHIO *mimes knocking on a door three times. At the same time, the* CHORUS *stomps three times on the floor, as if to make a "knocking" sound.*

HORTENSIO *wakes up and opens the door. He is happy to see*
PETRUCHIO.

HORTENSIO
> How now! My old friend Grumio!
> and my good friend Petruchio!
> What happy gale
> Blows you to Padua

ALL *onstage and offstage cheer.*

> here from old Verona?

HORTENSIO *greets them by grasping their forearms instead of*
shaking their hands.

PETRUCHIO
> Hortensio,
> I have thrust myself into this maze,
> Happily to wive and thrive, as best I may.

HORTENSIO *(looking at audience as if he has just had a great idea)*
> Petruchio, shall I then wish thee to
> a shrewd ill-favored wife?
> And yet I'll promise thee she shall be rich.
> > *(rubs fingers together)*

PETRUCHIO
> Signior Hortensio, if thou know
> One rich enough to be Petruchio's wife
> Be she as foul as was Florentius' love, makes an
> > ugly face
> were she as rough
> As are the swelling Adriatic seas *(staggers as if on*
> > *a boat in high waves and winds)*

I come to wive it wealthily in Padua;
If wealthily, then happily in Padua.
(rubs fingers together and smiles)

GRUMIO *(to* **HORTENSIO***)*
Why, give him gold enough
and marry him to an
old trot with ne'er a tooth in her head,
(makes an ugly face with a gummy smile)
though she have as many diseases as two-and-fifty
horses. *(snorts and stomps like a horse)*

HORTENSIO
I can, Petruchio, help thee to a wife
With wealth enough, and young and beauteous,
(mimes an hourglass figure with hands)
Her only fault
Is that she is intolerable curst,
And shrewd, and froward, so beyond all measure,
I would not wed her for a mine of gold.

PETRUCHIO
Hortensio, peace. Thou know'st not gold's effect.
I will board her, though she chide as loud
As thunder when the clouds in autumn crack. *(looks
up and claps hands to mimic a thunderclap)*

HORTENSIO
Her name is Katherina Minola,

ALL *onstage yell in fear.*

Renowned in Padua

ALL *onstage cheer.*

for her scolding tongue.

PETRUCHIO
> I will not sleep, Hortensio, till I see her.

HORTENSIO *(putting arm around* **PETRUCHIO** *conspiratorially)*
> Tarry, Petruchio. I must go with thee,
> For in Baptista's keep my treasure is.
> His youngest daughter, beautiful Bianca.

ALL *onstage coo.*

> Therefore this order hath Baptista ta'en,
> That none shall have access unto Bianca

ALL *onstage coo.*

> Till Katherine the curst

ALL *onstage yell in fear.*

> have got a husband.

HORTENSIO
> Now shall my friend Petruchio do me grace
> And offer me disguised in sober robes
> To old Baptista as a schoolmaster
> Well seen in music, to instruct Bianca,

GRUMIO *looks as though he has a great idea. He runs to grab a guitar from under his bench. He proudly hands the guitar to* **HORTENSIO.**

> That so I may, by this device at least,
> Have leave and leisure to make love to her.

ALL *exit back to their benches with* **HORTENSIO** *strumming the guitar,* **PETRUCHIO** *swaggering, and* **GRUMIO** *dancing a jig.*

✳ SCENE 3 (ACT II, SCENE I)

Padua, at the home of BAPTISTA.

Enter KATHERINE *and* BIANCA *from their benches.* BIANCA'S *hands are tied.*

BIANCA
> Good sister, wrong me not,
> Unbind my hands, I'll pull them off myself,
> Or what you will command me will I do,
> So well I know my duty to my elders.

KATHERINE
> Of all thy suitors here I charge thee tell
> Whom thou lov'st best.

BIANCA
> I prithee, sister Kate, untie my hands.

KATHERINE *strikes her.*

Enter BAPTISTA *from his bench. He unties* BIANCA'S *hands.*

BAPTISTA (*to* KATHERINE)
> For shame, thou hilding of a devilish spirit!

KATHERINE *chases after* BIANCA.

BAPTISTA
> What, in my sight?—Bianca, get thee in.

Exit BIANCA *to her bench.*

KATHERINE
> What, will you not suffer me? Nay, now I see
> She is your treasure, she must have a husband,
> I must dance barefoot on her wedding day
> And, for your love to her, lead apes in hell.

Exit KATHERINE *to her bench.*

BAPTISTA
> Was ever gentleman thus grieved as I?
> But who comes here?

Enter PETRUCHIO *from his bench.*

BAPTISTA
> God save you, gentleman.

PETRUCHIO
> And you, good sir. Pray, have you not a daughter
> Called Katherina, fair and virtuous?

BAPTISTA
> I have a daughter, sir, called Katherina.

PETRUCHIO
> I am a gentleman of Verona, sir,
> That hearing of her beauty and her wit,
> Am bold to show myself a forward guest
> Within your house
> Petruchio is my name.
> Tell me, if I get your daughter's love,
> What dowry shall I have with her to wife?

BAPTISTA

> After my death, the one half of my lands,
> And, in possession, twenty thousand crowns.

PETRUCHIO

> I tell you, father,
> I am as peremptory as she proud-minded;
> And where two raging fires meet together,
> They do consume the thing that feeds their fury.
> So I to her and so she yields to me,
> For I am rough and woo not like a babe.
> O, how I long to have some chat with her!

BAPTISTA

> Shall I send my daughter Kate to you?

PETRUCHIO

> I pray you do. I'll attend her here,

Exit **BAPTISTA** *to his bench.*

> And woo her with some spirit when she comes!
> Say that she rail, why then I'll tell her plain
> She sings as sweetly as a nightingale.
> Say that she frown, I'll say she looks as clear
> As morning roses newly washed with dew.
> But here she comes—and now, Petruchio, speak.

As if at a pro-wrestling match, **ALL** *on either side of the stage root for and support their respective "fighters." Those on stage right (***GRUMIO, HORTENSIO,*** and* **CHORUS***) root for* **PETRUCHIO***; those on stage left (***BAPTISTA, BIANCA, LUCENTIO, GREMIO,*** and* **CHORUS***) root for* **KATHERINE***.*

Enter **KATHERINE** *from her bench. One member of the* **CHORUS** *acts as her trainer and towels her down between rounds.*

KATHERINE *circles around* PETRUCHIO, *scowling and checking him out.*

GRUMIO *serves as* PETRUCHIO'S *trainer, looking in his eyes and toweling him off as if at a boxing match.*

PETRUCHIO *follows* KATHERINE *with his eyes. They stare at each other.*

A CHORUS *member plays "ding" on the triangle.*

Another CHORUS *member parades across the stage, holding a sign that says "Round 1."*

KATHERINE *walks to stage left, and* PETRUCHIO *walks to stage right. They turn and begin walking toward each other. With each step they take, a drumbeat and a quiet rattle sound from a* CHORUS *member.*

PETRUCHIO *(circling around* KATHERINE*)*
      Good morrow, Kate *(pauses)*, for that's your name,
        I hear.

KATHERINE
      Well have you heard, but something hard of hearing.
      They call me Katherine

ALL *onstage yell in fear.*

      that do talk of me.

PETRUCHIO
      You lie, in faith, for you are called plain Kate,
      And bonny Kate, and sometimes Kate the curst.
      But Kate, the prettiest Kate in Christendom,
      and therefore, Kate,

> Hearing thy mildness praised in every town,
> Thy virtues spoke of, and thy beauty sounded

KATHERINE *makes an ugly face at* PETRUCHIO.

> Myself am moved to woo thee for my wife.

PETRUCHIO *kneels, gently takes* KATHERINE'S *arm, and kisses her hand.*

KATHERINE
> "Moved," in good time! Let him that moved
>   you hither
> Remove you hence.

KATHERINE *knocks* PETRUCHIO'S *hat off his head.*

STAGE LEFT CHORUS *cheers for* KATHERINE.

CHORUS *member dings on triangle.*

CHORUS *member parades around the front of stage with a sign that says "Round 2."*

> I knew you at the first
> You were a movable.

PETRUCHIO *(moving to sit on stool)*
> Why, what's a movable?

KATHERINE
> A joint stool.

PETRUCHIO *is about to sit on stool when* KATHERINE *kicks it out from under him.* PETRUCHIO *falls to the ground.*

STAGE LEFT CHORUS *cheers for* KATHERINE.

PETRUCHIO *gracefully rolls off the ground and sits back on stool.*

PETRUCHIO
> Thou hast hit it. Come, sit on me.

PETRUCHIO *grabs* KATHERINE *and pulls her onto his lap.*

STAGE RIGHT CHORUS *cheers for* PETRUCHIO.

KATHERINE
> Asses are made to bear, and so are you.

KATHERINE *struggles to escape* PETRUCHIO'S *grip.*

STAGE LEFT CHORUS *mockingly say, "Oooo!" as if they have scored a point with their verbal prowess.*

PETRUCHIO
> Women are made to bear, and so are you.
> Come, come, you wasp! I' faith, you are too angry.

KATHERINE
> If I be waspish, best beware my sting.

KATHERINE *takes her finger and sticks it in* PETRUCHIO'S *eye.*

STAGE LEFT CHORUS *cheers for* KATHERINE.

KATHERINE *stands and walks stage left.*

PETRUCHIO *(following her)*
> Who knows not where a wasp does wear his sting?
> In his tail.

KATHERINE
> In his tongue. *(sticking her tongue out at him)*

PETRUCHIO
> Whose tongue?

KATHERINE
> Yours, if you talk of tales, and so farewell.

KATHERINE *starts to walk stage right, but* PETRUCHIO *runs in front of her.*

PETRUCHIO
> What, with my tongue in your tail?
> Nay, come again, good Kate. I am a gentleman.

KATHERINE
> That I'll try.

KATHERINE *strikes* PETRUCHIO.

CHORUS *member dings on triangle.*

STAGE LEFT CHORUS *cheers for* KATHERINE.

PETRUCHIO (*holding her arms*)
> I swear I'll cuff you if you strike again.

KATHERINE
> So may you lose your arms
> If you strike me, you are no gentleman,
> And if no gentleman, why then no arms.

KATHERINE *wrestles away from* PETRUCHIO.

PETRUCHIO
> A herald, Kate? O, put me in thy books.
> Opens his arms and kneels

KATHERINE
> What is your crest? A coxcomb?

PETRUCHIO
> A combless cock, so Kate will be my hen.

STAGE RIGHT CHORUS *makes clucking sounds like a chicken and flaps their wings.*

CHORUS *member dings on triangle.*

STAGE RIGHT CHORUS *laughs.*

KATHERINE
> No cock of mine. You crow too like a craven.

KATHERINE *comes face to face with* **PETRUCHIO.**

PETRUCHIO *grabs* **KATHERINE** *and stands behind her.*

CHORUS *member dings on triangle.*

STAGE RIGHT CHORUS *cheers for* **PETRUCHIO. STAGE LEFT CHORUS** *boos.*

> Let me go. *(struggles)*

PETRUCHIO
> No, not a whit. I find you passing gentle.
> 'Twas told me you were rough, and coy, and sullen,
> And now I find report a very liar.
> For thou art pleasant, gamesome, passing courteous,
> But slow in speech,

PETRUCHIO *puts his hand over* **KATHERINE'S** *mouth.* **KATHERINE** *bites his hand.*

> yet sweet as springtime flowers.

PETRUCHIO *and* KATHERINE *return to their corners.*

STAGE RIGHT CHORUS *encourages* PETRUCHIO *to go back for one more round.*

PETRUCHIO *and* KATHERINE *take one step toward each other with each sentence.*

With each step they take, a drumbeat and a quiet rattle sound from a CHORUS *member.*

KATHERINE
> Where did you study all this goodly speech?

PETRUCHIO
> It is extempore, from my mother wit.

KATHERINE
> A witty mother, witless else her son.

PETRUCHIO
> Am I not wise?

KATHERINE
> Yes, keep you warm.

KATHERINE *and* PETRUCHIO *are now circling each other slowly, facing each other.*

PETRUCHIO
> Marry, so I mean, sweet Katherine, in thy bed.
> And, will you, nill you, I will marry you.
> For I am he am born to tame you, Kate,
> And bring you from a wild Kate to a Kate
> Conformable as other household Kates.
> Give me thy hand, Kate. I will unto Venice

We will have rings, and things, and fine array,
And kiss me, Kate. We will be married o' Sunday.

KATHERINE *leans in as if to kiss* PETRUCHIO. PETRUCHIO *leans in, thinking he is going to kiss her.* KATHERINE *stomps on his foot, and one* CHORUS *member simultaneously makes a honking sound with a bike horn.*

✳ SCENE 4. (ACT III, SCENE I)

Padua, at the home of BAPTISTA.

Enter NARRATOR *from stage rear, coming downstage center.*

NARRATOR
> In an effort to win Bianca's hand, Lucentio disguises himself as a Latin teacher named Cambio. Hortensio disguises himself as a music teacher named Litio.

Enter BIANCA *from her bench, walking to center stage.*

Enter LUCENTIO *as* CAMBIO *from his bench. He stands to* BIANCA'S *left and holds a book.*

Enter HORTENSIO *as* LITIO *from his bench. He stands to* BIANCA'S *right and holds a guitar.*

NARRATOR
> Clever!

Exit NARRATOR *to bench.*

BIANCA
> Why, gentlemen, you do me double wrong
> To strive for that which resteth in my choice.
> I'll learn my lessons as I please myself.
> And, to cut off all strife, here sit we down.

BIANCA *sits on stool.* LUCENTIO *kneels next to her.*

BIANCA

> *(to* **HORTENSIO***)* Take you your instrument,
>> play you the whiles;
> His lecture will be done ere you have tuned.

HORTENSIO *begrudgingly takes a few steps stage right to tune his guitar.*

LUCENTIO *(aside)*

> That will be never: *(to* **HORTENSIO***)* Tune
>> your instrument.

BIANCA *(to* **LUCENTIO***)*

> Where left we last?

LUCENTIO

> Here, madam. *(showing her a book)*

LUCENTIO

> "Hic ibat," as I told you before, I am
> Lucentio, "hic est," son unto Vincentio of Pisa,
>> disguised thus to get your love,
> "Hic steterat," and that Lucentio that comes
>> a-wooing.

HORTENSIO *(coming back to* **BIANCA***)*
> Madam, 'tis now in tune.

HORTENSIO *plays again. It sounds terrible.*

BIANCA *and* **LUCENTIO** *cover their ears.* **BIANCA** *waves him away to continue tuning.*

BIANCA *(to* **LUCENTIO***)*
> In time I may believe, yet I mistrust.

HORTENSIO *comes back and puts himself between* BIANCA *and* LUCENTIO.

HORTENSIO *(to* LUCENTIO*)*
> You may go walk, and give me leave awhile.

LUCENTIO *steps aside, observing* HORTENSIO *jealously.*

LUCENTIO
> Well, I must wait
> *(aside)* And watch withal, for, but I be deceived,
> Our fine musician groweth amorous.

HORTENSIO
> Madam, before you touch the instrument,
> Yet read the gamut of Hortensio.

HORTENSIO *gives* BIANCA *a paper.*

BIANCA *(reading)* (**CHORUS** *joins her, simultaneously singing*
> *"do," "re," "mi," and "fa.")*
> "Do" I am, the ground of all accord:
> "re," to plead Hortensio's passion;
> "mi," Bianca, take him for thy lord,
> "fa" that loves with all affection;
> Call you this "gamut"? Tut, I like it not.
> Old fashions please me best. I am not so nice
> To change true rules for odd inventions.
> Tomorrow is my sister's wedding day.
> Farewell, sweet masters both. I must be gone.

LUCENTIO
> Faith, mistress, then I have no cause to stay.

BIANCA *and* LUCENTIO *exchange a long, loving look, which* HORTENSIO *notices. He is annoyed.*

Exit ALL *to their benches except* PETRUCHIO, *who exits stage right to put on his "outrageous" wedding garb offstage.*

✳ SCENE 5. (ACT III, SCENE II)

Padua, in front of the Church.

CHORUS *and* **KATHERINE** *stand and dance around the stage in a circle, some playing tambourines, as they chant, "The wedding, the wedding, of Petruchio and Katherina."*

KATHERINE *sits on stool center stage, looking frustrated.*

Once the wedding party assembles, there is an uncomfortable silence as everyone looks around for **PETRUCHIO**, *who has not arrived.*

BAPTISTA (to **TRANIO**)
  This is the 'pointed day
  That Katherine and Petruchio should be married,

ALL *cheer.*

  And yet we hear not of our son-in-law?

ALL *say,* "Aww."

KATHERINE *(pacing about the stage)*
  (addressing **WEDDING PARTY***)* I told you, I, he
    was a frantic fool,
  Hiding his bitter jests in blunt behavior,
  Now must the world point at poor Katherine
  And say "Lo, there is mad Petruchio's wife,
  If it would please him come and marry her!"

Exit **KATHERINE** *to her bench, weeping.*

BIONDELLO *stands from his bench and runs to stage right, looking offstage for* PETRUCHIO. *He returns to center stage to speak to* ALL.

BIONDELLO
> Why, Petruchio is coming

ALL *cheer.*

> in a new hat and
> an old jerkin,

ALL *say, "Huh?"*

> a pair of old breeches thrice turned,

ALL *say, "Eh?"*

> a pair of boots,
> one buckled, another laced;

ALL *say, "Whuh?"*

> an old rusty sword
> with a broken hilt, and
> a woman's crupper of velour.

ALL *react. Some might be in disgust, some in surprise, some in delight! The* CHORUS *can also react as one. See Performance Notes.*

> A monster,
> a very monster in apparel.

Enter GRUMIO *from his bench and* PETRUCHIO *from stage left, having changed his costume.*

PETRUCHIO (*looking around*)
>But where is Kate? Where is my lovely bride?
>(*to* BAPTISTA) How does my father? Gentles,
>>methinks you frown.

BAPTISTA
>Why, sir, you know this is your wedding day.
>First were we sad, fearing you would not come,
>Now sadder that you come
>An eyesore to our solemn festival.

PETRUCHIO
>Sufficeth I am come to keep my word,
>But where is Kate? 'Tis time we were at church.
>To me she's married, not unto my clothes.

Exit PETRUCHIO *with* GRUMIO *stage right.*

ALL *look around and exit, hurriedly following* PETRUCHIO *in the same order they entered, again chanting, "The wedding, the wedding, of Petruchio and Katherina."*

GREMIO *and* TRANIO *remain on stage while the wedding party goes around backstage and re-enters stage left.*

TRANIO
>Signior Gremio, came you from the church?

GREMIO
>As willingly as e'er I came from school.

TRANIO
>And is the bride and bridegroom coming home?

GREMIO
>Why, he's a devil, a devil, a very fiend.

TRANIO

> Why, she's a devil, a devil, the devil's dam.

GREMIO

> Such a mad marriage never was before!
> Hark, hark, I hear the minstrels play.

CHORUS *re-enters from stage right, dancing and chanting,*
"They're married, they're married, Petruchio and Katherina!"

PETRUCHIO *walks to center stage and stands on stool.*

PETRUCHIO *(grandiosely)*

> Gentlemen and friends, I thank you for your pains.
> I know you have prepared great store of wedding
>   cheer,
> But I mean to take my leave.
> I thank you all,
> That have beheld me give away myself
> To this most patient, sweet, and virtuous wife.

KATHERINE *(angrily and desperately)*

> Now, if you love me, stay.

PETRUCHIO

> Grumio, my horse.

GRUMIO

> Ay, sir, they be ready; the oats have eaten the horses.

KATHERINE *(crossing her arms)*

> Nay, then,
> Do what thou canst, I will not go today.
> The door is open, sir. There lies your way.
>   *(points stage right)*

PETRUCHIO *draws his sword, as does* **GRUMIO.**

PETRUCHIO takes KATHERINE by the arm and holds his sword out to defend himself from BAPTISTA and HORTENSIO, who approach him to "save" KATHERINE but back off when PETRUCHIO and GRUMIO brandish swords.

PETRUCHIO

>Nay, look not big, nor stamp, nor stare, nor fret;
>I will be master of what is mine own.
>She is my goods, my chattels; she is my house,
>My horse, my ox, my ass, my anything.
>And here she stands, touch her whoever dare.

Exit PETRUCHIO and KATHERINE stage right, with GRUMIO.

ALL laugh long and heartily.

BAPTISTA

>Nay, let them go. A couple of quiet ones!

GREMIO *(laughing)*

>I should die with laughing.

TRANIO *(also laughing)*

>Of all mad matches never was the like.

LUCENTIO

>Mistress, what's your opinion of your sister?

BIANCA

>That being mad herself, she's madly mated.

GREMIO

>I warrant him, Petruchio is Kated.

ALL exit to benches.

✳ SCENE 6. (ACT IV, SCENE I)

Padua, the home of PETRUCHIO.

Enter PETRUCHIO *from stage right, practically dragging a disheveled* KATHERINE, *accompanied by* GRUMIO.

PETRUCHIO
> Where be these knaves? What, no man at door
> To hold my stirrup nor to take my horse?

SERVANTS *(one each hopping up from the four benches)*
> Here, sir.

GRUMIO *walks behind* PETRUCHIO *to help remove his cape, but* PETRUCHIO *does not see him.*

PETRUCHIO
> Where is the foolish knave I sent before?

GRUMIO
> Here, sir, as foolish as I was before.

PETRUCHIO *is startled by* GRUMIO *and gives a yelp.*

PETRUCHIO *(backing* GRUMIO *around the stage angrily)*
> You peasant swain, you whoreson malt-horse
> drudge!
> Did I not bid thee meet me in the park
> And bring along these rascal knaves with thee?
> Go, rascals, go, and fetch my supper in!

Exit SERVANTS *to their benches to retrieve their props.*

> *(sings)* Where is the life that late I led?
> Sit down, Kate, and welcome.

KATHERINE *sits on stool;* PETRUCHIO *lolls on floor.*

Re-enter SERVANTS *from their benches, one with a hunk of meat on a bone, one with two plates, one with two cups, and one with silverware. They set the goods on the benches.*

> Why, when, I say?—Nay, good sweet Kate, be merry.
> Off with my boots, you rogues, you villains! When?

Two SERVANTS *pull at* PETRUCHIO'S *left boot; the other two* SERVANTS *pull at the right boot. It doesn't work. One* SERVANT *holds a second* SERVANT'S *waist, who then holds* PETRUCHIO'S *waist. The two remaining* SERVANTS *try pulling off the boots again.*

> Out, you rogues! You pluck my foot awry.

PETRUCHIO *motions for the servants to line up, which they do.*

> Take that!

PETRUCHIO *slaps the* SERVANTS *one by one. Each in turn slaps the next in line.*

The final SERVANT *has nobody to slap, so she looks left, then right, shrugs, and slaps herself.*

> Where are my slippers? Shall I have some water?

Exit SERVANTS *to their benches.*

Re-enter SERVANTS. *Two hold one slipper each, one holds a dish, and one holds a jug of water.*

> Come, Kate, and wash,

Two **SERVANTS** *rush to put the dish and water down for*
KATHERINE *to wash. They bump into each other and fall. The*
other two **SERVANTS** *try to help, but they also bump into each*
other and fall.

You whoreson villains, will you let it fall?

PETRUCHIO *starts kicking one* **SERVANT** *on the ground.* **KATHERINE**
stands and tries to help the **SERVANT.**

KATHERINE *(attempting to calm* **PETRUCHIO** *down)*
Patience, I pray you, 'twas a fault unwilling.

PETRUCHIO
A whoreson beetle-headed flap-eared knave!
Come, Kate, sit down. I know you have a stomach.
What's this? Mutton?

SERVANTS *(one at a time)*
Ay.

KATHERINE *is about to take a bite of the meat when* **PETRUCHIO**
grabs it just before it reaches her mouth.

PETRUCHIO
'Tis burnt, and so is all the meat.
There, take it to you, trenchers,

PETRUCHIO *throws the food and dishes at the* **SERVANTS.** *They*
run to pick up everything.

You heedless joltheads.

Each **SERVANT** *runs to the bench where they began the scene.*

KATHERINE (*starving*)
> I pray you, husband,
> The meat was well.

PETRUCHIO
> I tell thee, Kate, 'twas burnt and dried away,
> And for this night we'll fast for company.
> Come, I will bring thee to thy bridal chamber.

Exit PETRUCHIO *to his bench, taking a very frustrated*
KATHERINE.

Re-enter SERVANTS *from their benches, tiptoeing.*

GRUMIO (*to* SERVANTS)
> Didst ever see the like?

SERVANTS (*in unison*)
> He kills her in her own humor!

Exit SERVANTS *to their benches.*

Enter PETRUCHIO *from his bench.*

PETRUCHIO
> Thus have I politicly begun my reign.
> She ate no meat today, nor none shall eat.
> Last night she slept not, nor tonight she shall not.
> This is a way to kill a wife with kindness.
> And thus I'll curb her mad and headstrong humor.
> He that knows better how to tame a shrew,
> Now let him speak; 'tis charity to shew.

Exit PETRUCHIO *to his bench.*

✳ SCENE 7. (ACT V, SCENE II)

Padua, the home of LUCENTIO.

CHORUS *stands and dances around the stage, chanting, "The party, the party, of Petruchio and Katherina."*

ALL *form a semicircle upstage center, facing audience. There are three couples:* LUCENTIO *and* BIANCA *in the middle,* PETRUCHIO *and* KATHERINE *on the right, and* HORTENSIO *and* WIDOW *on the left.* BAPTISTA *stands to the right of* PETRUCHIO.

LUCENTIO

> At last, though long, our jarring notes agree
> And time it is when raging war is done
> To smile at 'scapes and perils overblown.
> My fair Bianca, bid my father welcome,
> While I with selfsame kindness welcome thine.
> Brother Petruchio, sister Katherina,
> And thou, Hortensio, with thy loving widow,
> Feast with the best, and welcome to my house.

BAPTISTA

> Now, in good sadness, son Petruchio,
> I think thou hast the veriest shrew of all.

Exit BIANCA, KATHERINE, *and* WIDOW *to the downstage right corner of the stage, insulted by that comment.*

PETRUCHIO

> Well, I say no. And therefore, for assurance,
> Let's each one send unto his wife,

And he whose wife is most obedient
To come at first when he doth send for her
Shall win the wager which we will propose.

HORTENSIO

Content, what's the wager?

LUCENTIO

A hundred crowns.

HORTENSIO

Content.

PETRUCHIO

A match! 'Tis done.

LUCENTIO (*to* BIONDELLO)

Go, Biondello, bid your mistress come to me.

BIONDELLO

I go.

Exit BIONDELLO *quickly downstage right to query* BIANCA.
BIONDELLO *appears to be asking* BIANCA *a question, and she
shakes her head "no."*

Re-enter BIONDELLO *immediately.*

LUCENTIO

How now, what news?

BIONDELLO (*to* LUCENTIO)

Sir, my mistress sends you word
That she is busy, and she cannot come.

LUCENTIO *appears shocked, embarrassed, and dismayed.*

ALL *laugh, mocking him.*

PETRUCHIO *(laughing, mocking)*
How? "She's busy, and she cannot come"?
Is that an answer?

GREMIO
Ay, and a kind one, too.
Pray God, sir, your wife send you not a worse.

HORTENSIO
Sirrah Biondello, go and entreat my wife
To come to me forthwith.

Exit **BIONDELLO** *quickly to* **WIDOW** *downstage right with other women.* **WIDOW** *also shakes her head "no."*

Re-enter **BIONDELLO**.

HORTENSIO *(haltingly, stuttering)*
Now, where's my wife?

BIONDELLO
She says you have some goodly jest in hand.
She will not come. She bids you come to her.

ALL *laugh, mocking* **HORTENSIO**, *who is embarrassed and flustered.*

PETRUCHIO *(amused)*
Worse and worse. She will not come!
O vile, intolerable, not to be endured!
Sirrah Grumio, go to your mistress,
Say I command her come to me.

Exit **GRUMIO** *toward the women downstage right.*

Enter KATHERINE *with* BIANCA *and* WIDOW *from downstage right.*

KATHERINE

What is your will, sir, that you send for me?

BAPTISTA

Now fair befall thee, good Petruchio!
For she is changed as she had never been.

PETRUCHIO

Nay, I will show more sign of her obedience,
Her new-built virtue and obedience.
Katherine, that cap of yours becomes you not.
Off with that bauble, throw it underfoot.

KATHERINE *obeys and throws the cap under her own foot,
grinding it into the ground.*

BIANCA

Fie, what a foolish duty call you this?

LUCENTIO

I would your duty were as foolish too.
The wisdom of your duty, fair Bianca,
Hath cost me a hundred crowns since suppertime.

BIANCA

The more fool you for laying on my duty.

PETRUCHIO

Katherine, I charge thee tell these headstrong
            women
What duty they do owe their lords and husbands.

WIDOW

Come, come. You're mocking. We will have no telling.

KATHERINE
> Fie, fie! Unknit that threat'ning unkind brow,
> And dart not scornful glances from those eyes
> To wound thy lord, thy king, thy governor.
> Thy husband is thy lord, thy life, thy keeper,
> Thy head, thy sovereign, one that cares for thee,
> Such duty as the subject owes the prince,
> Even such a woman oweth to her husband;
> I am ashamed that women are so simple
> But that our soft conditions and our hearts
> Should well agree with our external parts?
> *(to women onstage and in audience)* Come, come,
> you froward and unable worms!
> My mind hath been as big as one of yours,
> My heart as great, my reason haply more,
> To bandy word for word and frown for frown;
> But now I see our lances are but straws,
> Our strength as weak, our weakness past compare,
> That seeming to be most which we indeed least are.
> Then vail your stomachs, for it is no boot,
> And place your hands below your husband's foot;
> In token of which duty, if he please,
> My hand is ready, may it do him ease.

KATHERINE *puts her hand down on the ground, and* PETRUCHIO *puts his foot gently on it.*

PETRUCHIO
> Why, there's a wench! Come on, and kiss me, Kate.

KATHERINE *and* PETRUCHIO *kiss.*

ALL *stand and form a circle facing outward.*

(From Induction, Scene II)

ALL
>We all have come to play a pleasant comedy
>Seeing too much sadness hath congealed
>>your blood,
>Therefore we thought it good you hear a play
>Which bars a thousand harms and lengthens life!

ALL *hold hands and take a bow. Exeunt.*

✳ PERFORMING SHAKESPEARE

HOW *THE 30-MINUTE SHAKESPEARE* WAS BORN

In 1981 I performed a "Shakespeare Juggling" piece called "To Juggle or Not To Juggle" at the first Folger Library Secondary School Shakespeare Festival. The audience consisted of about 200 Washington, D.C. area high school students who had just performed thirty-minute versions of Shakespeare plays for each other and were jubilant over the experience. I was dressed in a jester's outfit, and my job was to entertain them. I juggled and jested and played with Shakespeare's words, notably Hamlet's "To be or not to be" soliloquy, to very enthusiastic response. I was struck by how much my "Shakespeare Juggling" resonated with a group who had just performed Shakespeare themselves. "Getting" Shakespeare is a heady feeling, especially for adolescents, and I am continually delighted at how much joy and satisfaction young people derive from performing Shakespeare. Simply reading and studying this great playwright does not even come close to inspiring the kind of enthusiasm that comes from performance.

Surprisingly, many of these students were not "actor types." A good percentage of the students performing Shakespeare that day were part of an English class which had rehearsed the plays during class time. Fifteen years later, when I first started directing plays in D.C. public schools as a Teaching Artist with the Folger Shakespeare Library, I entered a ninth grade English class as a guest and spent two or three days a week for two or three months preparing students for the Folger's annual Secondary School Shakespeare Festival. I have conducted this annual residency with the Folger ever since. Every year for seven action-packed days, eight groups of students between grades seven and twelve tread the boards onstage at the Folger's Elizabethan Theatre, a grand recreation of a sixteenth-century venue with a three-tiered gallery, carved oak columns, and a sky-painted canopy.

As noted on the Folger website (www.folger.edu), "The festival is a celebration of the Bard, not a competition. Festival commentators—drawn from the professional theater and Shakespeare education communities—recognize exceptional performances, student directors, and good spirit amongst the students with selected awards at the end of each day. They are also available to share feedback with the students."

My annual Folger Teaching Artist engagement, directing a Shakespeare play in a public high school English class, is the most challenging and the most rewarding thing I do all year. I hope this book can bring you the same rewards.

GETTING STARTED

GAMES

How can you get an English class (or any other group of young people, or even adults) to start the seemingly daunting task of performing a Shakespeare play? You have already successfully completed the critical first step, which is buying this book. You hold in your hand a performance-ready, thirty-minute cutting of a Shakespeare play, with stage directions to get the actors moving about the stage purposefully. But it's a good idea to warm the group up with some theater games.

One good initial exercise is called "Positive/Negative Salutations." Students stand in two lines facing each other (four or five students in each line) and, reading from index cards, greet each other, first with a "Positive" salutation in Shakespeare's language (using actual phrases from the plays), followed by a "negative" greeting.

Additionally, short vocal exercises are an essential part of the preparation process. The following is a very simple and effective vocal warm-up: Beginning with the number two, have the whole group count to twenty using increments of two (i.e., "Two, four, six . . ."). Increase the volume slightly with each number, reaching top volume with "twenty," and then decrease the volume while counting back down, so that the students are practically whispering when they arrive again at "two." This exercise teaches dynamics and allows them to get loud as a group without any individual pressure. Frequently during a rehearsal period, if a student is mumbling inaudibly, I will refer back to this exercise as a reminder that we can and often do belt it out!

"Stomping Words" is a game that is very helpful at getting a handle on Shakespeare's rhythm. Choose a passage in iambic pentameter and have the group members walk around the room in a circle, stomping their feet on the second beat of each line:

Two **house**-holds, **both** a-**like** in **dig**-nity
In **fair** Ve-**rona Where** we **lay** our **scene**

Do the same thing with a prose passage, and have the students discuss their experience with it, including points at which there is an extra beat, etc., and what, if anything, it might signify.

I end every vocal warm-up with a group reading of one of the speeches from the play, emphasizing diction and projection, bouncing off consonants, and encouraging the group members to listen to each other so that they can speak the lines together in unison. For variety I will throw in some classic "tongue twisters" too, such as, "The sixth sheik's sixth sheep is sick."

The Folger Shakespeare Library's website (http://www.folger.edu) and their book series *Shakespeare Set Free,* edited by Peggy O'Brien, are two great resources for getting started with a performance-based teaching of Shakespeare in the classroom. The Folger website has numerous helpful resources and activities, many submitted by teachers, for helping a class actively participate in the process of getting to know a Shakespeare play. For more simple theater games, Viola Spolin's *Theatre Games for the Classroom* is very helpful, as is one I use frequently, *Theatre Games for Young Performers*.

HATS AND PROPS

Introducing a few hats and props early in the process is a good way to get the action going. Hats, in particular, provide a nice avenue for giving young actors a non-verbal way of getting into character. In the opening weeks, when students are still holding onto their scripts, a hat can give an actor a way to "feel" like a character. Young actors are natural masters at injecting their own personality into what they wear, and even small choices made with how a hat is worn (jauntily, shadily, cockily, mysteriously) provide a starting point for discussion of specific characters, their traits, and their relationships with other characters. All such discussions always lead back to one thing: the text. "Mining the text" is consistently the best strategy for uncovering the mystery of Shakespeare's language. That is where all the answers lie: in the words themselves.

WHAT DO THE WORDS MEAN?

It is essential that young actors know what they are saying when they recite Shakespeare. If not, they might as well be scat singing, riffing on sounds and rhythm but not conveying a specific meaning. The real question is: What do the words mean? The answer is multifaceted, and can be found in more than one place. The New Folger Library paperback editions of the plays themselves (edited by Barbara Mowat and Paul Werstine, Washington Square Press) are a great resource for understanding Shakespeare's words and passages and "translating" them into modern English. These editions also contain chapters on Shakespeare's language, his life, his theater, a "Modern Perspective," and further reading. There is a wealth of scholarship embedded in these wonderful books, and I make it a point to read them cover to cover before embarking on a play-directing project. At the very least, it is a good idea for any adult who intends to direct a Shakespeare play with a group of students to go through the explanatory notes that appear on the pages facing the text. These explanatory notes are an indispensable "translation tool."

The best way to get students to understand what Shakespeare's words mean is to ask them what they think they mean. Students have their own associations with the words and with how they sound and feel. The best ideas on how to perform Shakespeare often come directly from the students, not from anybody else's notion. If a student has an idea or feeling about a word or passage, and it resonates with her emotionally, physically, or spiritually, then Shakespeare's words can be a vehicle for her feelings. That can result in some powerful performances!

I make it my job as director to read the explanatory notes in the Folger text, but I make it clear to the students that almost "anything goes" when trying to understand Shakespeare. There are no wrong interpretations. Students have their own experiences, with some shared and some uniquely their own. If someone has an association with the phrase "canker-blossom," or if the words make that student or his character feel or act a certain way, then that is the "right" way to decipher it.

I encourage the students to refer to the Folger text's explanatory notes and to keep a pocket dictionary handy. Young actors must attach some meaning to every word or line they recite. If I feel an actor is glossing over a word, I will stop him and ask him what he is saying. If he doesn't know, we will figure it out together as a group.

PROCESS VS. PRODUCT

The process of learning Shakespeare by performing one of his plays is more important than whether everybody remembers his lines or whether somebody misses a cue or an entrance. But my Teaching Artist residencies have always had the end goal of a public performance for about 200 other students, so naturally the performance starts to take precedence over the process somewhere around dress rehearsal in the students' minds. It is my job to make sure the actors are prepared—otherwise they will remember the embarrassing moment of a public mistake and not the glorious triumph of owning a Shakespeare play.

In one of my earlier years of play directing, I was sitting in the audience as one of my narrators stood frozen on stage for at least a minute, trying to remember her opening line. I started scrambling in my backpack below my seat for a script, at last prompting her from the audience. Despite her fine performance, that embarrassing moment is all she remembered from the whole experience. Since then I have made sure to assign at least one person to prompt from backstage if necessary. Additionally, I inform the entire cast that if somebody is dying alone out there, it is okay to rescue him or her with an offstage prompt.

There is always a certain amount of stage fright that will accompany a performance, especially a public one for an unfamiliar audience. As a director, I live with stage fright as well, even though I am not appearing on stage. The only antidote to this is work and preparation. If a young actor is struggling with her lines, I make sure to arrange for a session where we run lines over the telephone. I try to set up a buddy system so that students can run lines with their peers, and this often works well. But if somebody does not have a "buddy," I will personally make the time to help out myself. As I assure my students from the outset, I am not going to let them fail or embarrass themselves. They need an experienced leader. And if the leader has experience in teaching but not in directing Shakespeare, then he needs this book!

It is a good idea to culminate in a public performance, as opposed to an in-class project, even if it is only for another classroom. Student actors want to show their newfound Shakespearian thespian skills to an outside group, and this goal motivates them to do a good job. In that respect, "product" is important. Another wonderful bonus to performing a play is that it is a unifying group effort. Students learn teamwork. They learn to give focus to another actor when he is speaking, and to play off of other characters. I like to end each performance with the entire cast reciting a passage in unison. This is a powerful ending, one that reaffirms the unity of the group.

SEEING SHAKESPEARE PERFORMED

It is very helpful for young actors to see Shakespeare performed by a group of professionals, whether they are appearing live on stage (preferable but not always possible) or on film. Because an entire play can take up two or more full class periods, time may be an issue. I am fortunate because thanks to a local foundation that underwrites theater education in the schools, I have been able to take my school groups to a Folger Theatre matinee of the play that they are performing. I always pick a play that is being performed locally that season. But not all group leaders are that lucky. Fortunately, there is the Internet, specifically YouTube. A quick YouTube search for "Shakespeare" can unearth thousands of results, many appropriate for the classroom.

The first "Hamlet" result showed an 18-year-old African-American actor on the streets of Camden, New Jersey, delivering a riveting performance of Hamlet's "The play's the thing." The second clip was from *Cat Head Theatre,* an animation of cats performing Hamlet. Of course, YouTube boasts not just alley cats and feline thespians, but also clips by true legends of the stage, such as John Gielgud and Richard Burton. These clips can be saved and shown in classrooms, providing useful inspiration.

One advantage of the amazing variety of clips available on YouTube is that students can witness the wide range of interpretations for any given scene, speech, or character in Shakespeare, thus freeing them from any preconceived notion that there is a "right" way to do it. Furthermore, modern interpretations of the Bard may appeal to those who are put off by the "thees and thous" of Elizabethan speech.

By seeing Shakespeare performed either live or on film, students are able to hear the cadence, rhythm, vocal dynamics, and pronunciation of the language, and they can appreciate the life that other actors breathe into the characters. They get to see the story told dramatically, which inspires them to tell their own version.

PUTTING IT ALL TOGETHER

THE STEPS

After a few sessions of theater games to warm up the group, it's time to begin the process of casting the play. Each play cutting in *The 30-Minute Shakespeare* series includes a cast list and a sample program, demonstrating which parts have been divided. Cast size is generally between twelve and thirty students, with major roles frequently assigned to more than one performer. In other words, one student may play Juliet in the first scene, another in the second scene, and yet another in the third. This will distribute the parts evenly so that there is no "star of the show." Furthermore, this prevents actors from being burdened with too many lines. If I have an actor who is particularly talented or enthusiastic, I will give her a bigger role. It is important to go with the grain—one cast member's enthusiasm can be contagious.

I provide the performer of each shared role with a similar head-piece and/or cape, so that the audience can keep track of the characters. When there are sets of twins, I try to use blue shirts and red shirts, so that the audience has at least a fighting chance of figuring it out! Other than these costume consistencies, I rely on the text and the audience's observance to sort out the doubling of characters. Generally, the audience can follow because we are telling the story.

Some participants are shy and do not wish to speak at all on stage. To these students I assign non-speaking parts and technical roles such as sound operator and stage manager. However, I always get everybody on stage at some point, even if it is just for the final group speech, because I want every group member to experience what it is like to be on a stage as part of an ensemble.

CASTING THE PLAY

Young people can be self-conscious and nervous with "formal" auditions, especially if they have little or no acting experience.

I conduct what I call an "informal" audition process. I hand out
a questionnaire asking students if there is any particular role that
they desire, whether they play a musical instrument. To get a feel for
them as people, I also ask them to list one or two hobbies or inter-
ests. Occasionally this will inform my casting decisions. If someone
can juggle, and the play has the part of a Fool, that skill may come in
handy. Dancing or martial arts abilities can also be applied to roles.

For the auditions, I do not use the cut script. I have students
stand and read from the Folger edition of the complete text in order
to hear how they fare with the longer passages. I encourage them to
breathe and carry their vocal energy all the way to the end of a long
line of text. I also urge them to play with diction, projection, modu-
lation, and dynamics, elements of speech that we have worked on in
our vocal warm-ups and theater games.

I base my casting choices largely on reading ability, vocal strength,
and enthusiasm for the project. If someone has requested a particular role, I try to honor that request. I explain that even with a small
part, an actor can create a vivid character that adds a lot to the play.
Wide variations in personality types can be utilized: if there are two
students cast as Romeo, one brooding and one effusive, I try to put
the more brooding Romeo in an early lovelorn scene, and place the
effusive Romeo in the balcony scene. Occasionally one gets lucky, and
the doubling of characters provides a way to match personality types
with different aspects of a character's personality. But also be aware
of the potential serendipity of non-traditional casting. For example,
I have had one of the smallest students in the class play a powerful
Othello. True power comes from within!

Generally, I have more females than males in a class, so women are
more likely (and more willing) to play male characters than vice versa.

Rare is the high school boy who is brave enough to play a female character, which is unfortunate because it can reap hilarious results.

GET OUTSIDE HELP

Every time there is a fight scene in one of the plays I am directing, I call on my friend Michael Tolaydo, a professional actor and theater professor at St. Mary's College, who is an expert in all aspects of theater, including fight choreography. Not only does Michael stage the fight, but he does so in a way that furthers the action of the play, highlighting character's traits and bringing out the best in the student actors. Fight choreography must be done by an expert or somebody could get hurt. In the absence of such help, super slow-motion fights are always a safe bet and can be quite effective, especially when accompanied by a soundtrack on the boom box.

During dress rehearsals I invite my friend Hilary Kacser. a Washington-area actor and dialect coach for two decades. Because I bring her in late in the rehearsal process, I have her direct her comments to me, which I then filter and relay to the cast. This avoids confusing the cast with a second set of directions. This caveat only applies to general directorial comments from outside visitors. Comments on specific artistic disciplines such as dance, music, and stage combat can come from the outside experts themselves.

If you work in a school, you might have helpful resources within your own building, such as a music or dance teacher who could contribute their expertise to a scene. If nobody is available in your school, try seeking out a member of the local professional theater. Many local performing artists will be glad to help, and the students are usually thrilled to have a visit from a professional performer.

LET STUDENTS BRING THEMSELVES INTO THE PLAY

The best ideas often come from the students themselves. If a young actor has a notion of how to play a scene, I will always give that idea a try. In a rehearsal of *Henry IV, Part 1*, one traveler jumped into the other's arms when they were robbed. It got a huge laugh. This was something that they did on instinct. We kept that bit for the performance, and it worked wonderfully.

As a director, you have to foster an environment in which that kind of spontaneity can occur. The students have to feel safe to experiment. In the same production of *Henry IV*, Falstaff and Hal invented a little fist bump "secret handshake" to use in the battle scene. The students were having fun and bringing parts of themselves into the play. Shakespeare himself would have approved. When possible I try to err on the side of fun because if the young actors are having fun, then they will commit themselves to the project. The beauty of the language, the story, the characters, and the pathos will follow.

There is a balance to be achieved here, however. In that same production of *Henry IV, Part 1*, the student who played Bardolph was having a great time with her character. She carried a leather wineskin around and offered it up to the other characters in the tavern. It was a prop with which she developed a comic relationship. At the end of our thirty-minute *Henry IV, Part 1*, I added a scene from *Henry IV, Part 2* as a coda: The new King Henry V (formerly Falstaff's drinking and carousing buddy Hal) rejects Falstaff, banishing him from within ten miles of the King. It is a sad and sobering moment, one of the most powerful in the play.

But at the performance, in the middle of the King's rejection speech (played by a female student, and her only speech), Bardolph offered her flask to King Henry and got a big laugh, thus not only upstaging the King but also undermining the seriousness and poignancy of the whole scene. She did not know any better; she was bringing herself to the character as I had been encouraging her to do. But it was inappropriate, and in subsequent seasons, if I foresaw something like that happening as an individual joyfully occupied a character, I attempted to prevent it. Some things we cannot predict. Now I make sure to issue a statement warning against changing any of the blocking on show day, and to watch out for upstaging one's peers.

FOUR FORMS OF ENGAGEMENT: VOCAL, EMOTIONAL, PHYSICAL, AND INTELLECTUAL

When directing a Shakespeare play with a group of students, I always start with the words themselves because the words have the power to engage the emotions, mind, and body. Also, I start with the words in action, as in the previously mentioned exercise, "Positive and Negative Salutations." Students become physically engaged; their bodies react to the images the words evoke. The words have the power to trigger a switch in both the teller and the listener, eliciting both an emotional and physical reaction. I have never heard a student utter the line "Fie! Fie! You counterfeit, you puppet you!" without seeing him change before my eyes. His spine stiffens, his eyes widen, and his fingers point menacingly.

Having used Shakespeare's words to engage the students emotionally and physically, one can then return to the text for a more reflective discussion of what the words mean to us personally. I always make sure to leave at least a few class periods open for discussion of the text, line by line, to ensure that students understand intellectually what they feel viscerally. The advantage to a performance-based teaching of Shakespeare is that by engaging students vocally, emotionally, and physically, it is then much easier to engage them intellectually because they are invested in the words, the characters, and the story. We always start on our feet, and later we sit and talk.

SIX ELEMENTS OF DRAMA: PLOT, CHARACTER, THEME, DICTION, MUSIC, AND SPECTACLE

Over two thousand years ago, Aristotle's *Poetics* outlined six elements of drama, in order of importance: Plot, Character, Theme, Diction, Music, and Spectacle. Because Shakespeare was foremost a playwright, it is helpful to take a brief look at these six elements as they relate to directing a Shakespeare play in the classroom.

PLOT (ACTION)

To Aristotle, plot was the most important element. One of the purposes of *The 30-Minute Shakespeare* is to provide a script that tells Shakespeare's stories, as opposed to concentrating on one scene. In a thirty-minute edit of a Shakespeare play, some plot elements are necessarily omitted. For the sake of a full understanding of the characters' relationships and motivations, it is helpful to make short plot summaries of each scene so that students are aware of their characters' arcs throughout the play. The scene descriptions in the Folger editions are sufficient to fill in the plot holes. Students can read the descriptions aloud during class time to ensure that the story is clear and that no plot elements are neglected. Additionally, there are one-page charts in the Folger editions of *Shakespeare Set Free,* indicating characters' relations graphically, with lines connecting families and factions to give students a visual representation of what can often be complex interrelationships, particularly in Shakespeare's history plays.

Young actors love action. That is why *The 30-Minute Shakespeare* includes dynamic blocking (stage direction) that allows students to tell the story in a physically dramatic fashion. Characters' movements on the stage are always motivated by the text itself.

CHARACTER

I consider myself a facilitator and a director more than an acting teacher. I want the students' understanding of their characters to spring from the text and the story. From there, I encourage them to consider how their character might talk, walk, stand, sit, eat, and drink. I also urge students to consider characters' motivations, objectives, and relationships, and I will ask pointed questions to that end during the rehearsal process. I try not to show the students how I would perform a scene, but if no ideas are forthcoming from anybody in the class, I will suggest a minimum of two possibilities for how the character might respond.

At times students may want more guidance and examples. Over thirteen years of directing plays in the classroom, I have wavered between wanting all the ideas to come from the students, and deciding that I need to be more of a "director," telling them what I would like to see them doing. It is a fine line, but in recent years I have decided that if I don't see enough dynamic action or characterization, I will step in and "direct" more. But I always make sure to leave room for students to bring themselves into the characters because their own ideas are invariably the best.

THEME (THOUGHTS, IDEAS)

In a typical English classroom, theme will be a big topic for discussion of a Shakespeare play. Using a performance-based method of teaching Shakespeare, an understanding of the play's themes develops from "mining the text" and exploring Shakespeare's words and his story. If the students understand what they are saying and how that relates to their characters and the overall story, the plays' themes will emerge clearly. We always return to the text itself. There are a number of elegant computer programs, such as www.wordle.net, that will count the number of recurring words in a passage and illustrate them graphically. For example, if the word "jealousy" comes up more than any other word in *Othello,* it will appear in a larger font. Seeing the words displayed by size in this way can offer up illuminating insights into the interaction between words in the text and the play's themes. Your computer-minded students might enjoy searching for such tidbits. There are more internet tools and websites in the Additional Resources section at the back of this book.

I cannot overstress the importance of acting out the play in understanding its themes. By embodying the roles of Othello and Iago and reciting their words, students do not simply comprehend the themes intellectually, but understand them kinesthetically, physically, and emotionally. They are essentially *living* the characters' jealousy, pride, and feelings about race. The themes of appearance vs.

reality, good vs. evil, honesty, misrepresentation, and self-knowledge (or lack thereof) become physically felt as well as intellectually understood. Performing Shakespeare delivers a richer understanding than that which comes from just reading the play. Students can now relate the characters' conflicts to their own struggles.

DICTION (LANGUAGE)

If I had to cite one thing I would like my actors to take from their experience of performing a play by William Shakespeare, it is an appreciation and understanding of the beauty of Shakespeare's language. The language is where it all begins and ends. Shakespeare's stories are dramatic, his characters are rich and complex, and his settings are exotic and fascinating, but it is through his language that these all achieve their richness. This leads me to spend more time on language than on any other element of the performance.

Starting with daily vocal warm-ups, many of them using parts of the script or other Shakespearean passages, I consistently emphasize the importance of the words. Young actors often lack experience in speaking clearly and projecting their voices outward, so in addition to comprehension, I emphasize projection, diction, breathing, pacing, dynamics, coloring of words, and vocal energy. *Theatre Games for Young Performers* contains many effective vocal exercises, as does the Folger's *Shakespeare Set Free* series. Consistent emphasis on all aspects of Shakespeare's language, especially on how to speak it effectively, is the most important element to any Shakespeare performance with a young cast.

MUSIC

A little music can go a long way in setting a mood for a thirty-minute Shakespeare play. I usually open the show with a short passage of music to set the tone. Thirty seconds of music played on a boom box operated by a student can provide a nice introduction to the play, create an atmosphere for the audience, and give the actors a sense of place and feeling.

iTunes is a good starting point for choosing your music. Typing in "Shakespeare" or "Hamlet" or "jealousy" (if you are going for a theme) will result in an excellent selection of aural performance enhancers at the very reasonable price of ninety-nine cents each (or free of charge, see Additional Resources section). Likewise, fight sounds, foreboding sounds, weather sounds (rain, thunder), trumpet sounds, etc. are all readily available online at affordable cost. I typically include three sound cues in a play, just enough to enhance but not overpower a production. The boom box operator sits on the far right or left of the stage, not backstage, so he can see the action. This also has the added benefit of having somebody out there with a script, capable of prompting in a pinch.

SPECTACLE

Aristotle considered spectacle the least important aspect of drama. Students tend to be surprised at this since we are used to being bombarded with production values on TV and video, often at the expense of substance. In my early days of putting on student productions, I would find myself hamstrung by my own ambitions in the realm of scenic design.

A simple bench or two chairs set on the stage are sufficient. The sense of "place" can be achieved through language and acting. Simple set dressing, a few key props, and some tasteful, emblematic costume pieces will go a long way toward providing all the "spectacle" you need.

In the stage directions to the plays in *The 30-Minute Shakespeare* series, I make frequent use of two large pillars stage left and right at the Folger Shakespeare Library's Elizabethan Theatre. I also have characters frequently entering and exiting from "stage rear." Your stage will have a different layout. Take a good look at the performing space you will be using and see if there are any elements that can be incorporated into your own stage directions. Is there a balcony? Can characters enter from the audience? (Make sure that they can get there from backstage, unless you want them waiting in the lobby until their entrance, which may be impractical.) If possible, make sure to rehearse in that space a few times to fix any technical issues and perhaps discover a few fun staging variations that will add pizzazz and dynamics to your own show.

The real spectacle is in the telling of the tale. Wooden swords are handy for characters that need them. Students should be warned at the outset that playing with swords outside of the scene is verboten. Letters, moneybags, and handkerchiefs should all have plentiful duplicates kept in a small prop box, as well as with a stage manager, because they tend to disappear in the hands of adolescents. After every rehearsal and performance, I recommend you personally sweep the rehearsal or performance area immediately for stray props. It is amazing what gets left behind.

Ultimately, the performances are about language and human drama, not set pieces, props, and special effects. Fake blood, glitter, glass, and liquids have no place on the stage; they are a recipe for disaster, or, at the very least, a big mess. On the other hand, the props that are employed can often be used effectively to convey character, as in Bardolph's aforementioned relationship with his wineskin.

PITFALLS AND SOLUTIONS

Putting on a play in a high school classroom is not easy. There are problems with enthusiasm, attitude, attention, and line memorization, to name a few. As anybody who has directed a play will tell you, it is always darkest before the dawn. My experience is that after one or two days of utter despair just before the play goes up, show day breaks and the play miraculously shines. To quote a recurring gag in one of my favorite movies, *Shakespeare in Love:* "It's a mystery."

ENTHUSIASM, FRUSTRATION, AND DISCIPLINE

Bring the enthusiasm yourself. Feed on the energy of the eager students, and others will pick up on that. Keep focused on the task at hand. Arrive prepared. Enthusiasm comes as you make headway. Ultimately, it helps to remind the students that a play is fun. I try to focus on the positive attributes of the students, rather than the ones that drive me crazy. This is easier said than done, but it is important. One season, I yelled at the group two days in a row. On day two of yelling, they tuned me out, and it took me a while to win them back. I learned my lesson; since then I've tried not to raise my voice out of anger or frustration. As I grow older and more mature, it is important for me to lead by example. It has been years since I yelled at a student group. If I am disappointed in their work or their behavior, I will express my disenchantment in words, speaking from the heart as somebody who cares about them and cares about our performance and our experience together. I find that fundamentally, young people want to please, to do well, and to be liked. If there is a serious discipline problem, I will hand it over to the regular classroom teacher, the administrator, or the parent.

LINE MEMORIZATION

Students may have a hard time memorizing lines. In these cases, see if you can pair them up with a "buddy" and existing friend who will run lines with them in person or over the phone after school. If students do not have such a "buddy," I volunteer to run lines with them myself. If serious line memorization problems arise that cannot be solved through work, then two students can switch parts if it is early enough in the rehearsal process. For doubled roles, the scene with fewer lines can go to the actor who is having memorization problems. Additionally, a few passages or lines can be cut. Again, it is important to address these issues early. Later cuts become more problematic as other actors have already memorized their cues. I have had to do late cuts about twice in thirteen years. While they have gotten us out of jams, it is best to assess early whether a student will have line memorization problems, and deal with the problem sooner rather than later.

In production, always keep several copies of the script backstage, as well as cheat sheets indicating cues, entrances, and scene changes. Make a prop list, indicating props for each scene, as well as props that are the responsibility of individual actors. Direct the Stage Manager and an Assistant Stage Manager to keep track of these items, and on show days, personally double-check if you can.

In thirteen years of preparing an inner-city public high school English class for a public performance on a field trip to the Folger Secondary School Shakespeare Festival, my groups and I have been beset by illness, emotional turmoil, discipline problems, stage fright, adolescent angst, midlife crises (not theirs), and all manner of other emergencies, including acts of God and nature. Despite the difficulties and challenges inherent in putting on a Shakespeare play with a group of young people, one amazing fact stands out in my experience. Here is how many times a student has been absent for show day: Zero. Somehow, everybody has always made it to the show, and the show has gone on. How can this be? It's a mystery.

✳ PERFORMANCE NOTES: *THE TAMING OF THE SHREW*

This was my eighteenth consecutive year of conducting a teaching-artist residency in the D.C. Public Schools system, under the auspices of the Folger Shakespeare Library, and my first time staging a show in the round. This was not by choice. The Folger professional acting company was staging *Richard III* in the round, and performers at the Secondary School Shakespeare Festival at the Folger must stage their play on whatever set the Folger acting company is using at their Elizabethan theater.

In our production, all actors stayed on stage throughout the 30-minute performance, which was also a first for me. The students were seated on benches, four actors to a bench, with a total of sixteen cast members. During their scenes, the actors simply stood up from their benches and performed in the playing area between the benches rather than entering from the wings.

When not up on their feet acting, the remaining cast members served as the Chorus, providing a vocal and physical group response to the action on the stage. This made for a lively and fast-paced production with full participation and a commedia dell'arte feel, which fit the setting of the village of Padua and the raucous mood of the play.

For the purposes of this cutting, I adjusted the placement of the benches to reflect proscenium seating. For the staging in this text, I placed two benches upstage right and two benches upstage left, with four actors on each bench. Should you wish to adjust the staging to include more entrances and exits from offstage, the script is easily adapted to conventional staging, and you can still keep the Chorus participation intact for times when more actors are on stage. I will say that for this play, having the acting company onstage for the whole show gave the production a momentum and zest that would have been diluted with more conventional staging.

I did encounter some sight line issues with my blocking, however. Because the play was in the round, when the Chorus stood on the sidelines, they impeded the view of the characters in the middle of the stage. A performance of this version of *The Taming of the Shrew* on a conventional proscenium stage will not have the same issues. If I ever stage something in the round again, I will be more aware of this visibility issue and space my actors farther apart during crowd scenes, moving them closer to the "corners" of the playing area.

The Taming of the Shrew is a merry, madcap romp, and one that young actors relish. It is a challenge to stage due to the sheer physicality of the Kate-Petruchio interchanges. We worked slowly and methodically, taking great care to make sure all the "fight" scenes were safe. Ultimately, it was a great group effort and a spirited time featuring one of Shakespeare's best-matched pair of warriors in the battle of the sexes: Petruchio and Kate.

SCENE 1 (ACT I, SCENE I)

The scene begins with a merry Italian accordion tune played on a small portable stereo. For our student production, the stereo initially malfunctioned, leaving a confused and scrambling cast offstage, waiting for the sound issue to be resolved. Next time, I will address the possibility of technical difficulties and instruct the students to ignore malfunctioning equipment and simply enter with energy! It is more important for the performance to get underway than for a sound cue to work, but young actors need to have these contingencies spelled out for them ahead of time. As a bumper sticker of mine says: "Plan to improvise."

The play starts out with a bang. There is a drumroll, and Biondello runs onstage, gazing back offstage in a panic. A shoe flies over his head as a Chorus member blows into a siren whistle. A bearded, old Gremio runs on (with his cane), followed by Bianca and then Baptista, each actor fleeing an airborne shoe. The Chorus screams each time a shoe flies over their heads. Finally, as a Chorus member plays two ominous notes on the recorder, Katherine slowly walks around the circle of Chorus members, glaring at them. Bianca cowers behind her father, Baptista. Katherine lunges first at a Chorus member and then at an audience member. The mood is set.

Although we only use a drum, a recorder, and a siren for our sound effects, the timing of each sound greatly enhances the theatricality of our raucous entrance—and unlike the stereo, these instruments do not require batteries. When given a choice between pre-recorded music and live music played by cast members, always choose live music. The student who played the recorder had to learn basic fingering and blowing. I provided her with some instruction, but if you do not know how to play the instrument in question, YouTube is an endlessly helpful source of free tutorials.

The actress playing Katherine in this first scene was a spirited force: She grabbed Gremio's cane from him and waved it over his head threateningly as he hung onto Baptista to avoid falling down. There was nothing artificial looking about it. When one actor in a play or scene commits fully, the other actors rise to the same level of commitment.

Numerous running gags involving the Chorus recur throughout the first two scenes. The Chorus cheers and raises their arms in the air ("Hey!") each time the word "Padua" is uttered. They also coo "Aww" whenever Bianca's name is mentioned, which causes Bianca to stand from her chair and curtsy, acknowledging the applause. These repeated sound effects establish the Chorus as a character in the play.

After two scenes, we abandoned the "Hey!" and the "Aww" in favor of new Chorus cues because, like any running gag, we did not want to run it into the ground. I consult with the students to elicit their opinions during all phases of the staging process, which empowers them. Furthermore, they have great ideas.

SCENE 2 (ACT I, SCENE II)

We begin this scene with a silent vignette. Petruchio and Grumio come to Padua, steal some flowers from a flower vendor, and present them to a pair of village ladies. This is a short bit, but it establishes Petruchio as a rogue and Grumio as his sidekick. When Petruchio knocks on Lucentio's door, all Chorus members stomp their feet on the floor to create a "knocking" sound. This type of group sound effect takes some practice and concentration, but the effect of a unified Chorus is powerful and worth the effort to achieve.

Actors in a Shakespearean production must have an understanding of text and subtext and the ability to share that with the audience. When Petruchio exclaims to Lucentio that his intention is ". . . happily to wive and thrive," Lucentio looks out at the audience with a conspiratorial grin as if to say, "This might work out for me!" By conveying that he knows what Petruchio's words mean in the context of the story that is unfolding, the actor playing Lucentio brings the audience in on his journey. They want to know what he knows.

The study and performance of Shakespeare always starts with the words themselves. Encourage students to enjoy the way the words feel tripping off their tongues. Lucentio holds the guitar in his hand and gyrates like a Renaissance rock star as the alliterative line ". . . have leave and leisure to make love to her" leaves his lips. He then strums his out-of-tune guitar merrily as he, Petruchio, and Grumio dance off the stage. Shakespeare's words are fun to speak.

SCENE 3 (ACT II, SCENE I)

A great example of the power of the ensemble to punch up the drama occurred during this scene. Kate has tied Bianca's hands and is pulling her around the stage. The actress playing Bianca is in control here as her hands are not really tied; she has wrapped a rope around them and is leading the action. She decides when to fall on her knees. We had to move slowly and methodically during these "stage combat" scenes. If you have no experience with stage combat, please research it and find someone with experience to help you if you can.

With Bianca on her knees, Katherine reaches her hand back and slaps Bianca hard in the face. A great slapping sound accompanies the hit, and the audience responds with a loud "Ooh!" At the precise moment that Katherine's hand crossed the plane of Bianca's face, while never touching it, the Chorus clapped their hands together loudly. The audience did not expect it and reacted strongly. When Katherine exclaimed, "I must dance barefoot on her wedding day," and performed a little dance move with her hand over her head, the entire Chorus leaped to their feet, echoed the dance move, and yelled, "Whooah!" (Their choice of sound, of course.) Long live the power of the ensemble!

The battle of words in this scene between Kate and Petruchio is staged like a professional wrestling fight, complete with announcer ("Let's get ready to ruuuumble!"), a bell, and a Chorus member holding a card announcing the rounds ("Round 1," "Round 2"). Kate's fans gather on one side of the stage and Petruchio's fans on the other, cheering and booing each verbal hit.

Petruchio's repetition of the name "Kate" can be an opportunity for the actor playing Petruchio to experiment with different ways of saying her name: sweetly, curtly, mockingly, softly, or in a sing-song style. Each time he says her name, Petruchio can come right up to Kate's ear, pause, and then speak the name. I do not feel that we exploited the potential of this idea in our production, mostly because there was so much other blocking to achieve in this scene. We can seldom achieve all of our goals for a show when confronted with time limitations. On the other hand, we should keep trying right up until the last minute!

One key to success in this battle of the wits is for Kate and Petruchio to pick up on each other's cues quickly. In some scenes, "beats" provide breathing room for the audience to see the character's thought process or digest her words and ideas. Not so in this scene. It should be a back-and-forth lightning-speed word war. A funny and effective sound effect concludes the scene. Katherine appears to concede to Petruchio's "Kiss me Kate" command and allows him into her arms. She then stomps on his foot, which is accompanied by a Chorus member making a squeaky sound with a clown horn. That's comedy!

SCENE 4 (ACT III, SCENE I)

The young lady playing Cambio (Lucentio in disguise) in our production played the scene with amorous commitment, gently stroking Bianca's chin, leaning in, and whispering sweetly in her ear. There was a delightful seductiveness to her performance, and the choices were all hers. It is a blessing when an actor takes a small part and invests it with a large emotion—in this case, lust!

We found a commedia dell'arte mask for Litio (Hortensio in disguise) to wear for this scene. If you plan to introduce a mask, beard, or other potentially cumbersome prop or costume piece into a production, do so as early in the rehearsal process as possible. I introduced this mask a little late, and the actress spent a significant amount of time onstage trying to keep it from falling off. Nonetheless, it was a nice touch, and a nod to the commedia dell'arte style that we brought to the production.

Again, we used the Chorus to good effect in this scene. As Bianca sang the notes on the paper ("do," "re," "mi," etc.), the Chorus sang those notes in unison. After "fa," one Chorus member stood up and sang, "So!" in a loud voice. Realizing that she was all alone on that note, she then glanced about embarrassed, exclaimed, ". . . oh," and sat back down. One of the joys in staging a comedy is that we are constantly on the lookout for moments where we can get a laugh.

With everybody onstage at all times, we always had the personnel on hand to achieve that funny moment!

SCENE 5 (ACT II, SCENE II)

The scene begins with a chanting dance around the stage, complete with tambourines, drums, and hand claps: "The wedding, the wedding, of Petruchio and Katharina." During our performance, the audience clapped along joyously. The Chorus repeated the chant upon exiting the stage and returned a few seconds later, chanting, "They're married!" Repetition enhances comedy, especially when one employs the rule of three: 1) start a theme, 2) establish the theme by repeating it, and 3) break the theme by inserting an unexpected change. Adding to the comedy was the ridiculously short 30-second interval between the group's leaving the stage for the wedding and returning after it. Comedy can be absurd; conventional rules of time and space do not have to apply.

The actress playing Katherine in this scene chose to portray a genuinely despondent and heartbroken bride left at the altar. She cried and threw her flowers to the ground before slumping in her seat. Just because it is a comedy does not mean the emotions are not real. In fact, playing a character's negative feelings earnestly often serves a comedy better than mugging or creating a caricature of an emotion.

SCENE 6 (ACT IV, SCENE I)

Petruchio is genuinely angry and impatient in this scene, and at one point he erupts into violence, kicking a servant on the ground before the other servants intervene. This spurs Katherine on to her plaintive line, "Patience, I pray you, 'twas a fault unwilling." This provides the student playing Katherine an opportunity to show how she is changing from a headstrong, bellicose woman to one who has suffered and can show compassion.

We chose one servant in this scene to be the "slow" one, always arriving to say, "Here, sir," or serve the dish a little later than the other servants. The payoff for this setup occurred near the end of the scene when the servants exclaim in unison, "He kills her in her own humor!" Immediately after this, the "slow" servant came running up and repeated the line too late, which got a laugh from the audience.

We choreographed a piece of business wherein Petruchio slapped a servant, who subsequently slapped the next servant, who slapped the next, and so on down the line. The "slow" servant was at the end of the line, and so she looked around, saw nobody to slap, shrugged her shoulders, paused for a second, and then slapped herself. A huge laugh erupted from the audience. Even minor characters can have major comic moments if they look for them, rehearse them, time them out correctly, and exploit them.

SCENE 7 (ACT V, SCENE II)

The Chorus had an exceptionally good time making fun of Lucentio and Hortensio during this scene as they bid their wives to come and their wives refuse. Upon seeing Biondello return alone, the actor playing Hortensio gave out a plaintive stutter: "N…n…now, where's my wife?" That small comic adjustment paid off in a big laugh. Again, this was a stutter of the actor's choosing.

As director, I have to find a balance between suggesting actor's choices and letting the actors make their own choices. Invariably, the actors' own choices are superior. My real job is to encourage the process, and if that means suggesting a choice, I will do so. Sometimes it is better to brainstorm with the actor or the group to come up with several options on how to play a scene or a line. This demonstrates that there is no one way to play a part and that at every step of the way, an actor has choices.

Katherine's final speech is problematic for modern audiences. How are we to reconcile the line, "Thy husband is thy lord, thy life, thy keeper, thy head, thy sovereign" with the proud and wild Katherine of earlier in the play? The challenge is up to the actor to find something in the words that makes sense to her.

I encouraged the actor playing Katherine in this scene to study the speech and see if there were any words or phrases that she could apply to an aspect of her own life or her relationships. I shared with the class a few of my own personal interpretations based upon my own relationships, not just with my spouse but with other entities, some of them perhaps not human (e.g., God or Spirit). One beauty of Shakespeare's language is that it is poetic and opens itself up to interpretation on a number of levels. The words do not have to be taken literally; they might be interpreted metaphorically, ironically, humorously, or bitterly.

Ultimately, the student playing Katherine made her own choices, having studied other actors' versions of the speech on film, and thought about what the words meant to her personally. I believe our entire acting company as well as the audience left the theater with our own personal interpretation of *The Taming of the Shrew*. We also all left the theater with at least one experience in common: We laughed!

✳ *THE TAMING OF THE SHREW:* SET AND PROP LIST

SET PIECES:

Stool

Four benches (additional benches will be needed for a cast
of more than sixteen players)

PROPS:

THROUGHOUT FOR CHORUS:

Hand drum

Tambourine

Siren whistle

Rattle or maraca

Bike horn

Triangle or bell

SCENE 1:

Four shoes for Katherine to throw

Cane for Gremio

SCENE 2:

Flowers and basket for Flower Vendor

Fruit and basket for Fruit Vendor

Bag for Petruchio

Guitar for Hortensio

SCENE 3:

Rope for Bianca's hands

Bell or triangle

Cue cards reading "Round 1" and "Round 2"

Two towels for "trainers" in fight scene

SCENE 4:

Masks for Hortensio/Litio and Lucentio/Cambio

Guitar for Hortensio/Litio

Piece of paper for Hortensio/Litio to give to Bianca

Latin book for Lucentio/Cambio

SCENE 5:

Swords for Petruchio and Grumio

Outrageous hat/costume pieces for Petruchio's wedding outfit

SCENE 6:

Two plates, two cups, and silverware for Servants

Pair of slippers for Servants to offer to Petruchio

Jug of water for Servants

Fake piece of meat for Servants

The Taming of the Shrew
By William Shakespeare
Performed by Banneker Academic High School
Mr. Feeser's Twelfth Grade English Class

Folger Secondary School Shakespeare Festival | Monday, March 10th, 2014
Instructor: Mr. Charles Feeser | Guest Director: Mr. Nick Newlin

CAST:

Scene 1 (Act I, Scene 1)
Lucentio (Suitor to Bianca): Jason McKenzie
Tranio (Servant to Lucentio): Rosie Rodriguez
Baptista (Father to Katherine and Bianca):
Urael Asfaha
Gremio (Suitor to Bianca): Anaise Aristide
Katherine (Baptista's eldest daughter):
Chanel "Nelly-Nel" Smith!
Bianca (Baptista's younger daughter)
Neiel Edmonds

Scene 2 (Act I, Scene 2)
Petruchio (Suitor to Katherine):
Sierra Douglas Ph.D
Grumio (Servant to Petruchio):
Tierra Sales (The Joker) AKA Tee Tee
Hortensio (Suitor to Bianca):
"The" Ronald Arbertha Jr.

Scene 3 (Act II, Scene 1)
Bianca: Neiel Edmonds
Katherine: Chanel "Nelly-Nel" Smith!
Baptista: Urael Asfaha
Petruchio: Rashaad Purnell
Grumio/Petruchio's Hype: Tierra Sales
(The Joker) AKA Tee Tee
Gremio/Katherine's Hype: Anaise Aristide

Scene 4 (Act III, Scene 1)
Bianca: Neiel Edmonds
Hortensio (As Litio, A music teacher):
Cierra Nichols
Lucentio (As Cambio, A Latin teacher):
Blendia Moore

Scene 5: (Act III, Scene 2)
Baptista: Urael Asfaha
Katherine: Tiarra Goodwin
Biondello (Servant to Lucentio): Reniya Dinkins
Petruchio: Sierra Douglas Ph.D
Tranio: Rosie Rodriguez
Gremio: Anaise Aristide
Grumio: Tierra Sales (The Joker) AKA Tee Tee

Scene 6 (Act IV, Scene 1)
Petruchio: Sierra Douglas Ph.D
Grumio: Tierra Sales (The Joker) AKA Tee Tee
Katherine: Tiarra Goodwin
Servants: Reniya Dinkins, Blendia Moore,
Rosie Rodriguez, Cierra Nichols

Scene 7: (Act V, Scene 2)
Lucentio: Jason McKensie
Petruchio: Rashaad Purnell
Baptista: Urael Asfaha
Hortensio: "The" Ronald Arbertha Jr.
Biondello: Reniya Dinkins
Gremio: Anaise Aristide
Katherine: Nae Chantae
Bianca: Neiel Edmonds
Widow: Sydney Reynolds
Narrator: Nae Chantae
Boombox: Rashaad Purnell
Musicians/Sound Effects: "The" Ronald
Arbertha, Jr., Tiarra Goodwin, Rosie Rodriguez,
Reniya Dinkins, Sydney Reynolds, Blendia Moore,
Cierra Nichols, Chanel "Nelly-Nel" Smith

Stage Manager: Nae Chantae

"I am as peremptory as she proud-minded
And where two raging fires meet together
They do consume the thing that feeds their fury."
—Petruchio

ADDITIONAL RESOURCES

SHAKESPEARE

Shakespeare Set Free: Teaching Romeo and Juliet, Macbeth and a Midsummer Night's Dream
Peggy O'Brien, Ed., Teaching Shakespeare Institute
Washington Square Press
New York, 1993

Shakespeare Set Free: Teaching Hamlet and Henry IV, Part 1
Peggy O'Brien, Ed., Teaching Shakespeare Institute
Washington Square Press
New York, 1994

Shakespeare Set Free: Teaching Twelfth Night and Othello
Peggy O'Brien, Ed., Teaching Shakespeare Institute
Washington Square Press
New York, 1995

The *Shakespeare Set Free* series is an invaluable resource with lesson plans, activites, handouts, and excellent suggestions for rehearsing and performing Shakespeare plays in a classroom setting.

ShakesFear and How to Cure It!
Ralph Alan Cohen
Prestwick House, Inc.
Delaware, 2006

The Friendly Shakespeare: A Thoroughly Painless Guide to the Best of the Bard
Norrie Epstein
Penguin Books
New York, 1994

Brush Up Your Shakespeare!
Michael Macrone
Cader Books
New York, 1990

Shakespeare's Insults: Educating Your Wit
Wayne F. Hill and Cynthia J. Ottchen
Three Rivers Press
New York, 1991

Practical Approaches to Teaching Shakespeare
Peter Reynolds
Oxford University Press
New York, 1991

Scenes From Shakespeare:
A Workbook for Actors
Robin J. Holt
McFarland and Co.
London, 1988

101 Theatre Games for Drama
Teachers, Classroom Teachers
& Directors
Mila Johansen
Players Press Inc.
California, 1994

THEATER AND PERFORMANCE

Impro: Improvisation and the Theatre
Keith Johnstone
Routledge Books
London, 1982

A Dictionary of Theatre Anthropology:
The Secret Art of the Performer
Eugenio Barba and Nicola Savarese
Routledge
London, 1991

THEATER GAMES

Theatre Games for Young Performers
Maria C. Novelly
Meriwether Publishing
Colorado, 1990

Improvisation for the Theater
Viola Spolin
Northwestern University Press
Illinois, 1983

Theater Games for Rehearsal:
A Director's Handbook
Viola Spolin
Northwestern University Press
Illinois, 1985

PLAY DIRECTING

Theater and the Adolescent Actor:
Building a Successful School Program
Camille L. Poisson
Archon Books
Connecticut, 1994

Directing for the Theatre
W. David Sievers
Wm. C. Brown, Co.
Iowa, 1965

The Director's Vision: Play Direction
from Analysis to Production
Louis E. Catron
Mayfield Publishing Co.
California, 1989

INTERNET RESOURCES

http://www.folger.edu
The Folger Shakespeare Library's
website has lesson plans, primary
sources, study guides, images,
workshops, programs for teachers
and students, and much more. The
definitive Shakespeare website for
educators, historians and all lovers
of the Bard.

http://www.shakespeare.mit.edu.
The Complete Works of
William Shakespeare.
All complete scripts for *The
30-Minute Shakespeare* series were
originally downloaded from this site
before editing. Links to other internet
resources.

http://www.LoMonico.com/
Shakespeare-and-Media.htm
http://shakespeare-and-media
.wikispaces.com
Michael LoMonico is Senior
Consultant on National Education
for the Folger Shakespeare Library.
His *Seminar Shakespeare 2.0* offers a
wealth of information on how to use
exciting new approaches and online
resources for teaching Shakespeare.

http://www.freesound.org.
A collaborative database of sounds
and sound effects.

http://www.wordle.net.
A program for creating "word clouds"
from the text that you provide. The
clouds give greater prominence to
words that appear more frequently in
the source text.

http://www.opensourceshakespeare
.org.
This site has good searching capacity.

http://shakespeare.palomar.edu/
default.htm
Excellent links and searches

http://shakespeare.com/
Write like Shakespeare,
Poetry Machine, tag cloud

http://www.shakespeare-online.com/

http://www.bardweb.net/

http://www.rhymezone.com/
shakespeare/
Good searchable word and phrase
finder.
Or by lines:
http://www.rhymezone.com/
shakespeare/toplines/

http://shakespeare.mcgill.ca/
Shakespeare and Performance
research team

http://www.enotes.com/william-
shakespeare

Needless to say, the internet goes on and on with valuable Shakespeare resources.
The ones listed here are excellent starting points and will set you on your way in the
great adventure that is Shakespeare.

THE TAMING OF THE SHREW: THE 30-MINUTE SHAKESPEARE
SAMPLE BENCH CONFIGURATION

Four actors per bench

STAGE

STOOL

AUDIENCE

NUMBER OF BENCHES CAN BE INCREASED
WITH INCREASED CAST SIZE.

NICK NEWLIN has performed a comedy and variety act for international audiences for thirty-two years. Since 1996, he has conducted an annual play directing residency affiliated with the Folger Shakespeare Library in Washington, D.C. Newlin received a BA with Honors from Harvard University in 1982 and an MA in Theater with an emphasis in Play Directing from the University of Maryland in 1996.

THE 30-MINUTE SHAKESPEARE

AS YOU LIKE IT
978-1-935550-06-8

THE COMEDY OF ERRORS
978-1-935550-08-2

HAMLET
978-1-935550-24-2

HENRY IV, PART 1
978-1-935550-11-2

HENRY V
978-1-935550-38-9

JULIUS CAESAR
978-1-935550-29-7

KING LEAR
978-1-935550-09-9

LOVE'S LABOR'S LOST
978-1-935550-07-5

MACBETH
978-1-935550-02-0

A MIDSUMMER NIGHT'S DREAM
978-1-935550-00-6

THE MERCHANT OF VENICE
978-1-935550-32-7

THE MERRY WIVES OF WINDSOR
978-1-935550-05-1

MUCH ADO ABOUT NOTHING
978-1-935550-03-7

OTHELLO
978-1-935550-10-5

RICHARD III
978-1-935550-39-6

ROMEO AND JULIET
978-1-935550-01-3

THE TAMING OF THE SHREW
978-1-935550-33-4

THE TEMPEST
978-1-935550-28-0

TWELFTH NIGHT
978-1-935550-04-4

THE TWO GENTLEMEN OF VERONA
978-1-935550-25-9

THE 30-MINUTE SHAKESPEARE ANTHOLOGY
978-1-935550-33-4

All plays $9.95, available in print and eBook editions in bookstores everywhere

---

"A truly fun, emotional, and sometimes magical first experience . . . guided by a sagacious, knowledgeable, and intuitive educator." —Library Journal

PHOTOCOPYING AND PERFORMANCE RIGHTS

There is no royalty for performing any series of *The 30-Minute Shakespeare* in a classroom or on a stage. The publisher hereby grants unlimited photocopy permission for one series of performances to all acting groups that have purchased the play. If a group stages a performance, please post a comment and/or photo to our Facebook page; we'd love to hear about it!

9 781935 550334